HELLO
MY NAME IS
Edith
ASHLEYVILLE
P.T.A

A mom who understands

with love to

Jan

1981

hang in there, MOM

BY NOVA TRIMBLE ASHLEY
ILLUSTRATED BY MEL CRAWFORD

FOR MY CHILDREN
AND FOR THEIRS

ACKNOWLEDGMENTS

For permission to reprint certain of these poems in this collection, thanks are due
to the editors of Capper's Weekly, Denver Post, Farmland, Hallmark, Inc., Kansas
Farmer, McCall's, Midwest Chaparral, Mother's Manual, Ladies' Home Journal, PEN,
Reader's Digest, The Saturday Evening Post, Today's Christian Mother, The Villager,
Wall Street Journal, and others.

"Undercover Girl," "Dishing it Out," "Seasons' Leavings," "Live and in Color,"
"Father Attends a Musicale," "Spring Rains," and "Morning to Remember," by
permission of Good Housekeeping Magazine © 1970, 71, 72, 73, 74 by Hearst Corpora-
tion. And a very special thanks to Golden Quill Press for use of a few of these verses
from "Loquacious Mood."

hello baby

HER FIRSTLING

Released, she dozed with languid laziness,
Exhausted after labor, slightly shaken . . .
A squalling! Only then did haziness
Give way to consciousness, did she awaken
To innocence newborn with smoke-blue eyes
And quivering hunger-puckered rosebud lips
Demanding her . . . then did she realize
She was a mother to her fingertips!

COUNT YOUR BLESSINGS

Ten little fingers, ten little toes,
And two inquisitive eyes;
Two little ears and a button nose,
A mouth of diminutive size.

Two little feet and two little hands,
An exquisite bundle of joy;
With two big lungs at 2 a.m.—
Your eight-pound baby boy!

Hush! For our new baby daughter is sleeping,
Long curling lashes on rose petals lie;
Lips slightly puckered like buds that are kissing
Soft baby breath as it passes them by.
Look! Now our new baby daughter is smiling.
Angels are guarding her—there's no mistake!
Into her wee, shell-like ear they are whispering—
Who dares to question, to hint tummy ache?

Record of the pre-school child
From our modern annals:
First he learns to tell the hour—
Next, the TV channels.

A baby is able—
When left at the table
While mother must answer the door—
To toss, with a clatter,
His oatmeal; and splatter
In seconds, a newly-waxed floor.

A creeping cherub can be trusted
To travel where you haven't dusted
As he investigates the floors,
Manipulating on all fours.
Behind the sofa, first, he goes
And gathers lint between his toes;
Then scoots beneath a Windsor chair
Where cobwebs dangle from his hair.
He crawls along a what-not shelf
And deftly finger-prints himself . . .
Try as you may, there's just no stopping
A creeping moppet from dust-mopping.

BUSY TODDLER

She never walks! She seldom sits!
Her small demanding presence flits
Like dancing sunbeams all day long;
She races, with a little song
Upon her lips—she's never still,
She'll bounce into your heart . . .
She will.

A LITTLE BOY'S QUESTIONS

The questions little boys can ask!
Like: Do you have a notion
How many years the sun can last?
And did God pour the ocean?
And do we dream in SLOW or FAST?
And does a prayer have motion?
While he is young, it's good to bask
In such complete devotion!

INTERPRETER OF DREAMS

"Mommy, I had a dream last night!"
Cried wide-awake, small Sue,
"I dreamed I was a little girl . . .
With a Mommy just like you!"

"But, darling, you are my little girl;
And I'm your Mommy, too!"
She smiled, "Well, that just goes to show
How much my dreams come true!"

Our toddler has adoring aunties
Who fashion dolly duds with panties
Of handmade lace, an elfin bonnet
Of crêpe de Chine with rosebuds on it;
Soft blue chiffon for dolly's dress
To hide her cotton nakedness—
And velvet shoes! (One toe is missing,
But four are quite enough for kissing.)

Alas! These fancy frills and stitches
Are strewn about, from top to britches;
Ignored is dolly's pulchritude—
Preferred is dolly-in-the-nude;
Our child disrobes her babe, to spank it
And wrap it in a dog-eared blanket.
Bless aunties! But for Dolly-Squeezing,
Most toddlers go for stripper-teasing.

LAMENT TO MARCH

"In like a lion, out like a lamb"—
Or the other way around;
Little boys with doors to slam
Are much like March, I've found.

See how my three-year-old can write!
I wouldn't call it scribbling—
Although I know some folks who might,
But I'm not one for quibbling.

To some, these circles could be bugs;
These lines, just hits or misses—
But I know wobbly "O's" are hugs,
And crooked "X's," kisses!

A PICTURE OF CHILDHOOD

Jennifer is an artist.
(Jennifer is three.)
The lady with the purple hair
In corkscrew curls is me.

The green stick man is Daddy;
This glob of gray, the cat;
The milkman's done in yellow;
The postman's blue and fat.

She will do your portrait.
(Only takes a minute.)
A Jennifer Original
Has so much love within it.

10

He doesn't bring chocolates, lockets of gold,
Red roses, cologne of narcissus;
But he hands me a Christmas card, crumpled and old—
And I thank him with hugs and kisses.

It was one of those days! I couldn't begin
To count all my woes, I confess;
But I left my laundry to let her in,
And apologized for the mess.

The baby was crying, the dog wanted out;
I suppose I looked annoyed—
But why must a census taker shout:
"I see you're unemployed!"

LITTLE RAGAMUFFINS

Long summer hours our children play,
Scantily clad, barefoot and brown;
It's only at the close of day
We dress them up to bed them down.

INSTANT THIRST

Try doing dishes in your sink
When umpteen kiddies want a drink;
Or mop the kitchen—see who's first
To track the floor or die of thirst.

THE DISAPPEARING ACT

The sandbox is the place to look
For items like a buttonhook,
A baseball cap, a rubber shoe,
A spatula, a spoon or two,
A colander or, like as not,
The basket to your coffeepot.

But sand, itself, is seldom there—
You look for that in children's hair!

Little children, autumn eves,
Tend to go together—
Picking walnuts, kicking leaves,
Apple-crispy weather.

Little children, autumn nights,
Have a way of meeting;
Jack-o'-lanterns, bonfire lights,
Time for Trick-or-Treating.

Our children never lose their socks
Or sandals on the beach;
Or anything that comes in pairs—
They lose just one of each.

The Birthday Boy is pensive—
Six little guests are there;
And now with party ending,
The Birthday Boy must share.

The Birthday Mom is beaming;
And holding up for size,
Six squirming baby kittens—
Each guest has won a prize!

CHRISTMAS MOURNING

Our Junior is sobbing—
He can't find a part
To his train, and without it,
The engine won't start.

Our daughter is whining—
Just hear her complain:
She doesn't like dolls
And she wanted a train!

But baby is cooing—
Santa Claus brought him blocks;
And he's having a ball
With the nice, empty box.

ESPECIALLY ON RAINY DAYS

Children are active little things.
They shatter nerves like broken wings
Of night moths. They perplex
With questions, track in mud and vex
The neighbors. They delight
In teasing; or they scream and fight
Like elfin demons in a brawl,
Racing, shrieking, down the hall . . .
And yet—this makes me want to weep—
They look like angels in their sleep.

SPRING RAINS

Mothers, from the beginning of mud,
Have not resolved the riddle
Of why a puddle lures a child
To land right in the middle.

MORNING TO REMEMBER

The children have fixed a breakfast tray,
My special treat for Mother's Day.
The toast is charred, the coffee thin;
The chef, age six, wears an awkward grin
While little sister, with sober face,
Adds a droopy rose to a doll-size vase.
I smile at them, try not to think
Of sticky stove and splattered sink—
The kitchen will take an hour to clean,
But my heart will treasure, forever, this scene.

He skips beside me. I resolve to keep
Quite calm as Baby starts to nursery school.
I've heard old-fashioned mothers used to weep
Most unashamedly . . . but now the rule
Is smart sophistication. Surely I
Will not resort to acting like a fool!
But when he darts ahead and waves goodbye,
I turn my back and run . . . and cry and cry.

I'm president of the P.T.A.!
How did I ever make it?
I'm dedicated, qualified . . .
And no one else would take it.

DISHING IT OUT

When the kids sit down to dinner,
I don't ask them to applaud;
But they'll never pick a winner
With: "Look what Mom has thawed!"

THE "SPOILS" SYSTEM

The neighbor's kids are brassy—
The most obnoxious kind!
Our kids are never sassy—
They only speak their mind.

PHOTOGENIC CHILDREN

They wiggle and giggle
When I say "Cheese!"
But when I take movies,
They stand like trees.

AUTOMATION

Push buttons to wash,
Push buttons to dry;
If I could push children
With buttons, I'd try.

He settles in a folding chair,
Then glances at the clock.
Piano plinkings fill the air
With simulated Bach.

He hides a yawn, then folds his arms;
His presence here is vital
As little daughter flaunts her charms
At this, her first recital.

Our children loathe spinach,
They gag at the stuff—
Except at the neighbor's
They can't get enough!

Girls at slumber parties giggle,
Eat and chatter, scream and wiggle!
When there are two or more in number,
Slumber parties seldom slumber.

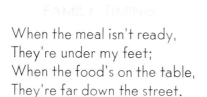

When the meal isn't ready,
They're under my feet;
When the food's on the table,
They're far down the street.

20

You pick a swanky place to eat
To give the kids a culture-treat.
They scan the menu, front to rear,
And wail, "I can't find hot dogs here!"

I won't sniff the bacon,
Punch the bread out of shape,
Or sample the peanuts
Or nibble a grape.

I won't squeeze the tissue,
Or do anything wrong;
At least, not this morning—
The kids are along.

When teen-age son or daughter
Comes bounding in with zest
And begs for errands, you can bet
They've passed their driver's test.

When I made him wear a jacket,
I thought sure my son would die!
He declared it was a racket
As I struggled with his tie.

When he left the house that morning,
He was grumbling all the while;
So I called a cheerful warning:
"Now remember, dear, to smile!"

Well, the photo came on Monday;
And my photogenic son
Is one in sixteen hundred—
But I can't decide which one!

Our teen-age son is fine so far!
No problem—if you please;
He never asks to use the car,
But only for the keys.

Our college daughter calls collect;
And every time she raves
About the rising cost of stamps
And all the cash she saves.

If your teen-age kids ignore you,
Just try not to be bitter;
In a few years they'll adore you—
When they need a baby-sitter.

"Hello! Yes, this is Mom . . . Yes, Son?
Oh! . . . Christmas at her mother's? . . .
Of course! She is their only one;
And as you say—we've others!
Now, Son, please don't apologize . . .
Perhaps another year? . . .
Of course I do! . . . I realize! . . .
And . . . Merry Christmas, dear!"

I thought he'd never say good-by
So I could take time out . . . to cry!

23

Some rooms are done in Danish mode;
Contemporary, French abode,
Colonial, or border
On modern Japanese decor;
But ours is none of these—it's more
Like Permanent Disorder!

A puppy's great for kids to own!
It fills their home with laughter
And mud and hair and half-gnawed bone . . .
For Mom to clean up after.

The paper boy was late again;
You think I'd be a dope
And blindly trust to fate again
Without my horoscope?

STOCKING UP

In grocery stores, I travel miles
All up and down the narrow aisles
For paper towels, laundry soaps,
Ball point pens and envelopes,
Magazines and potted plants,
Needles, thread and baby pants.
And when I'm loaded down with frills
Like dental cream and headache pills,
I check my list—it's quite complete . . .
Except for something we can eat.

She is perfect, but completely!—
Speaking softly, smiling sweetly,
Never screaming, nagging, fretting,
Scolding children for forgetting
Little things, a book, a jacket;
And she just adores their racket.

She is eager with her "Yessing,"
And my children, I'm confessing,
Quote her more than any other—
Everybody Else's mother.

EARTH MOTHER

Barefoot, I stand
In sifted sand.
Upon the shore?
No, bathroom floor.

SUMMER BLAST

Next week? The annual steak fry!
(We have a reservation);
And daughter plans a party
With endless preparation;
The Boy Scouts hold their circus
And son will man his station;
And I bought concert tickets
With keen anticipation . . .
Tonight my spouse announces:
"Surprise!—Next week's vacation!"

If modern fathers feel neglected,
Complaining they are not respected,
And wonder if it's worth the bother,
They should think of Whistler's father.

Our view is a sight full;
The children, non-hectic;
Our meals are delightful
Cooked on an electric.
Our quarters are coolish;
The mattresses, foam.
You may think it's foolish—
But we're staying home.

I have no patience in a line
Of shopping carts ahead of mine;
And so I spin my wheels and race . . .
Back and forth . . . to find a place.

When now my cart is far behind
I gnash my teeth, for there I find
The ones who waited patiently
are checking out . . . ahead of me!

Our mother used to say to us—
When summer days were fair—
"Why don't you children run outside
And get some nice fresh air?"

But now, with air-conditioned homes,
Polluted times like these,
I tell my kiddies, "Come inside
And get a little breeze!"

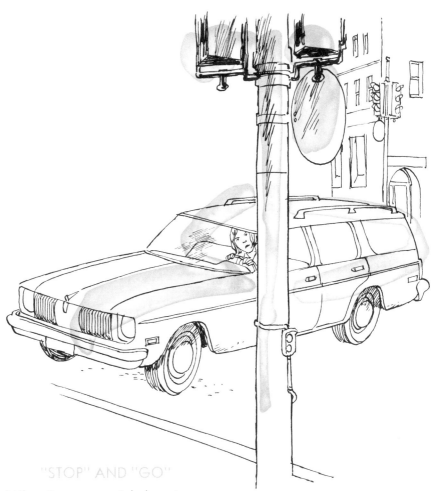

"STOP" AND "GO"

When I've no special place to go,
The streets are all serene—
The traffic zooms, a steady flow,
And all the lights turn green.

But when I have an urgent date,
The traffic snails ahead;
It's only when I know I'm late
That all the lights turn red.

Nothing so inspires me
To wash a load of clothes;
Or sprinkle down the flower beds
From the garden hose;
Or scrub the kitchen cupboards,
Or bathe a little daughter,
As when the plumber hollers:
"I'm turning off the water!"

SEASONS' LEAVINGS

There's nothing more embarrassing
Before your mother-in-law's eye,
Than emptying your sweeper bag
Of Christmas tinsel . . . in July!

BEHIND THE STEERING WHEEL

"Be careful, dear!" Why does he think
I'm doing things all wrong?
I'll never drive my spouse to drink . . .
He's scared to come along!

When I am dressed in Sunday best
For strolling through a store
Or down the street, I never meet
A soul I've seen before.

But let me race to marketplace
With curlers in my hair
And run-down heels—this trip reveals
My best-groomed friends are there.

I simply dread
To make a bed.
There isn't any
Doubt
The hardest part
Is when I start
By getting myself
Out.

These mirrors in a fitting room
Can send me into fits of gloom;
That's me in front—so never mind!
But who's that chubby gal behind?

Suspense has reached its highest peak;
But Mom and the kids should have known
That someone, sometime, would ask to speak
To **Dad** on the telephone.

I'm thankful for so many things—
But let me name just two:
When all the guests have taken wings,
And all the dishes through!

SLIM CHANCE

Resolve anew? I'll try it;
Once more I take my pen
To start the year with, "Diet!"
And close with, "Try again!"

WHAT COLOR ARE ANGELS?

"What color are angels?" my little girl queries,
"Can angels be yellow or purple or pink?"
I conjure up visions of golden-tressed cherubs
From Sunday School leaflets. But wait! Let me think:
Are they brown-sugar brown or cranberry red?
Are they licorice black, pudding lemon, or peach?
Or white as the icing on cakes, freshly spread?
What color **are** angels? I'd guess some of each!

ODE TO AUTUMN

Poets, from the time of old,
Lauded leaves of red and gold.
Poets, if I'm not mistaken,
Never had the job of rakin'!

I knitted a sweater
And when it was done,
Too small for my hubby,
Too large for my son,
I didn't unravel
Or toss on a shelf,
I added a ribbon
And wore it myself!

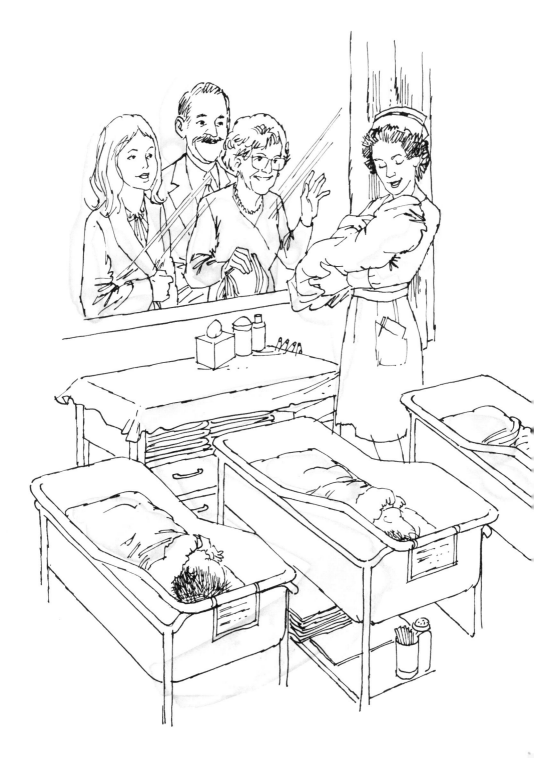

It must have happened times before—
To use a trite expression,
As many as the stars, or more—
But I've a wild confession:
That never, never until this
In all the family history
Could anyone have known such bliss
Or marveled at such mystery!

My heart flip-flops a jubilee—
They've pulled the nursery curtain;
It's happening to me, to me!
I'm grandmother now for certain!

Here is something to treasure,
To love beyond measure,
And to pamper, with pleasure . . .
A grandson!

LIVE AND IN COLOR

Turn off the stereo, turn off TV.
Our gala performance is something to see!
Phone the grandparents to rush on their way—
Baby is taking his first steps today.

GRANDMOTHER'S
SWEET CONSENSUS

She was the strictest mother!
Her children seldom munched
Or stuffed on cake and candy
Till after they had lunched.

Now she's a fond grandmother—
Still strict, you realize—
No cookies before mealtime . . .
Unless a grandchild cries!

Prettiest, dressed in a ruffled gown
And pony-tail, with those eyes so brown!
Flirtiest, sitting on Grandpa's lap;
Naughtiest, fighting her daily nap;
But happiest, clad in a worn-out pair
Of faded jeans, with the wind in her hair.

AFTER A WEEK'S VISIT
WITH GRANDMOTHER

Yesterday I welcomed my little boy back;
But today I'm beginning to rue it—
And tomorrow I'm liable to blow my stack
If he says, once more:
"Grandmother lets me do it!"

Little children, quickly gone,
Quickly climb the mountain stair;
Swiftly, too, the years move on . . .
Who can find the Fountain—where?
One by one they fly the nest,
Leaving empty places;
While we say, "It's for the best" . . .
Still, their little faces
Smile at us in reverie
When we trim the Christmas tree.

Motherhood's a most demanding task;
Patience is the order of the day;
And yet it's really great to be a Mom . . .
I wouldn't have it any other way.